The Shape of Golf, Plane and Simple

Bob Haas

First published by Dog Ear Publishing
4010 W. 86th Street, Ste H
Indianapolis, IN 46268
www.dogearpublishing.net

ISBN: 978-159858-564-3

This book is printed on acid-free paper.

Printed in the United States of America

OBSERVATION POINT

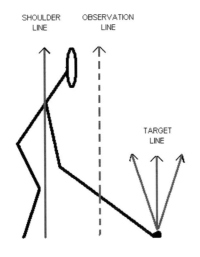

SHOULDER LINE   OBSERVATION LINE   TARGET LINE

To begin, stand behind the golfer to observe the golf swing from a line parallel to the shoulders and between the shoulders and the ball (the dotted line in the image). When you look down the observation line, it may be parallel to the target line, or it may be to the left or right of the target line. This is the best angle for observing THE SHAPE OF GOLF, and the following illustrations will be valid only from this vantage point. Any other vantage point will make THE SHAPE OF GOLF distorted. Standing behind the golfer from the correct position, which is the observation line, is the best observation position because it's easiest to see the ball flight, THE SHAPE OF GOLF, posture, and shoulder alignment.

Minimal time should be spent observing the swing from straight-on or while looking at only the front side of the swing, because the shape of the swing is too difficult to define. Only the up-and-down part of the swing can be observed from straight-on. It's two-dimensional, and THE SHAPE OF GOLF can't be observed from the straight-on point.

07.14.2007

2

07.14.2007

3

07.14.2007

4

BALL RELATIVE TO THE BODY

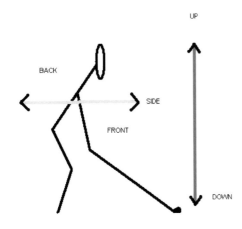

When a golfer swings a club, the golf ball is on the ground and in front of the body. The fact the ball is on the ground means that the club will need to swing up and down. The up-and-down of the swing is achieved by the arm swing. Up-and-down in a pure form would be similar to a Ferris wheel, but a golfer would have to stand on the target line to swing like that. Golfers stand to the side of the target line, which means the club must also swing side-to-side.

The side-to-side of the swing is achieved in two ways. First, the side-to-side is achieved by keeping the shoulders level while turning on the backswing and keeping a level turn-through of the hips and shoulders on the follow-through. Second, the side-to-side is achieved by properly rolling back the wrist on the backswing and properly rolling through the wrist on the follow-through. Side-to-side in a pure form would be like a baseball swing, which would work really well if the ball was on a 3-foot tee.

Combining the up and down action with the side to side action is what makes the golf swing so difficult. Furthermore, the golf club and the arms do not form a straight line. If they did form a straight line, then a club could be swung on a single arc or a perfect arc. An angle exists between the club and the arms. Therefore, a balanced arc should exist for consistency.

07.14.2007

6

07.14.2007

8

THE DUAL ARC ANGLE

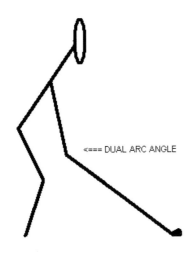

<=== DUAL ARC ANGLE

The fact that no straight line runs from the club head to the shoulder means that the club cannot swing on a single arc. An angle exists from the club to the arms. This angle can be referred to as the dual arc angle. From a geometric standpoint, one line would be able to work on one arc. But in golf, there are two lines, the arm and the club. Therefore, a number of arcs must exist.

The dual arc angle is responsible for THE SHAPE OF GOLF and establishes the roll or rotation of the wrist in the golf swing. The dual arc angle should remain the same for all golf clubs, which also makes the wrist rotation the same for all golf clubs. If this angle differs from one club to the next, then the rotation of the wrist would also have to differ, making the swing more inconsistent.

THE SINGLE ARC THEORY

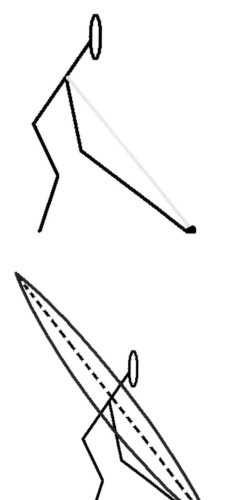

One line does not exist from the club head to the shoulder; if it did, you could swing the club in a single arc. Two lines are formed from the club head to the shoulders. The first line is the arm, and the second is the club shaft. If you swing the club in a single arc, your arms and the club would not be in balance. Remember, only one line can work on one arc.

The yellow line is a straight line from the club head to the shoulder. This can be swung on a single arc, which is the purple arc. Notice that a triangle exists from the yellow line to the arms to the club. This triangle exists with all great golfers at the set-up position. The ability for a golfer to create a straight line from the shoulder to the club head would be unnatural and nearly impossible, given the make-up of the human body and the way a golfer must grip the club. Trying to swing the club head on the purple line would make hitting the ball in the middle of the face more difficult and more random.

10

THE SINGLE ARC

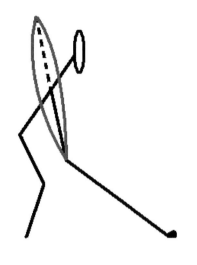

There's a single arc in the golf swing, and it's the one formed by the left arm and left shoulder. This arc has two fundamental parts, width and height. During the backswing, width is achieved by pulling back or turning back the shoulder. Width on the follow-through is achieved by the turning-through or pivot-through of the body. The height of the swing is achieved when the arms swing up and down.

The more level the body turns in the back-swing and follow-through, the more width a golfer will have. Tilting the shoulders on the backswing or follow-through may warp this arc. A degree of tilt may exist, but golfers don't want more than a degree. A perfect combination of turning back, turning through, and swinging the arms up and down is responsible for this arc.

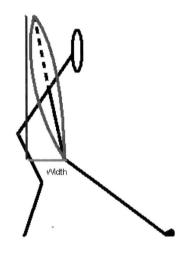

If a golfer doesn't turn but does swing the arms up and down, then too much height will exist. If a golfer turns too much and doesn't swing the arms up and down, then there will be too much width.

11

07.14.2007

12

THE SINGLE ARC CAN VARY

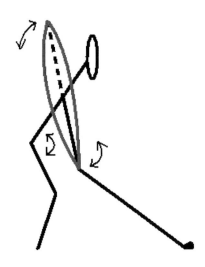

The single arc in the golf swing can vary. It may be more up and down (height), or it may be more side to side (width). The posture, which is the bend at the hips, can vary this arc. Posture is controlled by the length of the club, and all clubs vary in length, depending on which one a golfer uses. A golfer's physique will also vary this arc. Golfers with longer arms will have more width, and golfers with shorter arms will have more height. By using the same swing with more bend at the hips, this arc will have more height (short clubs). By using the same swing and less bend at the hips, this arc will have more width (long clubs).

07.14.2007

14

07.14.2007

15

SINGLE ARC IS FOR THE ARMS

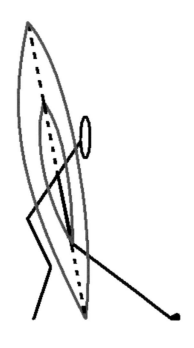

The single arc in THE SHAPE OF GOLF is for the arms to swing on. Do not swing the golf club on this arc. Golfers that swing the club on this arc will have a tendency to hit balls off the toe of the golf club. When studying the arc drawn, notice that when the arc is extended down below the dual arc angle, it returns inside the club head or to the left of the club at impact. If the club was swung on this arc, there would be no centrifugal force to move the club in front of the hands at impact. This arc is too vertical and would hit the ball off the toe of the club. A large number of amateur golfers hit the ball off the toe because they are too vertical. Or they try to swing the club on a single arc, which is also too vertical.

THE CLUB ARC

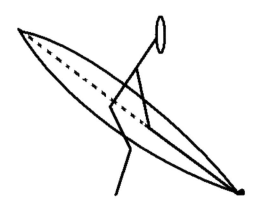

The golf club starts on this arc. For most golfers, this arc would be too flat or have too much width. Golfers using this arc would have to keep their backswings short of the full position. Pitching swings, which are swings short of the full position, can use this arc. Using this arc requires a wrist roll in the backswing. Trying to get the club and hands to swing on this arc would be difficult and would be too flat. This arc and the wrong posture would cause the ball to be stuck off the heel of the club.

TRUE SHAPE OF PURE GOLF

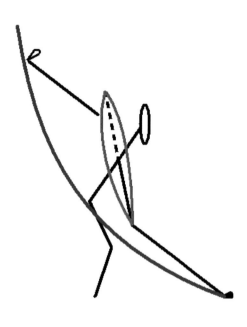

The following image shows the true shape of pure golf. This shape may be very likely the best way to swing a golf club. This form will have the highest probability of success and will provide the most efficient application of the club into the ball. A perfectly symmetrical in-to-in swing follows this shape and is the way to swing the club straight down the target line with a level angle of compression. The benefit of a balanced swing is perfect ball striking and hits in the middle of the clubface. Hitting the ball in the middle of the face is more important today than ever before because of the length of the modern day course. The ball speed will be highest when the ball is hit in the middle of the face. Modern day golfers must use this shape on the downswing, including professional golfers. However, you'll observe that their backswings sometimes vary.

This shape is achieved by pulling the shoulder back to get width on the inside arc. The arms swing up to give height to the inside arc. The wrist roll allows the club to rotate from in front to behind the inside arc. Since the inside arc is a perfect arc, the outside arc or blue line is a warped arc working from in front to behind a perfect arc.

07.14.2007

19

07.14.2007

20

07.14.2007

21

07. 14. 2007

22

07.14.2007

23

07.14.2007

24

PUTTING IT ALL TOGETHER

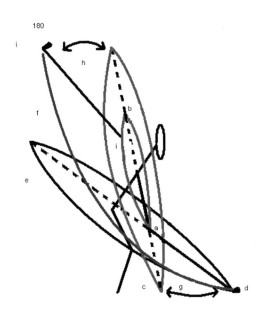

The dual arc angle starts the shape of the golf swing and is responsible for the development of the swing arc (a). The arms swing along the inside red arc (b). It is a single arc because the arm forms a straight line (one line, one arc). The club cannot swing on this arc because it is too up and down (c). The ball would be hit off the toe of the club if this arc was used (d). The club is not swung up the black line because it is too flat (e). The swing should use the blue arc, which the club stays on by rolling the wrist in the backswing. This arc is the balanced arc (f).

The blue arc is THE SHAPE OF GOLF, PLANE AND SIMPLE. Notice how the arc is balanced. The distance the club is in front of the hands (g) is equal to the distance the club is behind the hands (h) at the 180° position. The club has traveled 180°, but the hands have not (I). At the 180° position, the club head reaches its fullest height and width (j). In any arc, after the club head reaches the 180° position, it will change direction. This bal-

25

ance in the arc is the key to hitting the ball in the middle of the clubface, which is the key to consistency and distance. A wobble in this arc would create a random impact.

Most professional golfers that use the black arc on the backswing use shorter swings and reroute to the balanced arc. Because the club changes direction at the 180° position, if the black arc continues to the full position, the club will point to the right at the top of the swing. When the club points right, this is called "across the line." Many amateurs are plagued by getting the club across the line, which creates many bad swing habits. It is OK to let the club work behind the body early on the backswing, but it's not OK to let the hands work behind the body too early. The hands should work behind the body just below the right shoulder. Some professionals use the red or vertical arc on the backswing. They too must re-route the club back to the blue or balanced arc.

DUAL ARC 2

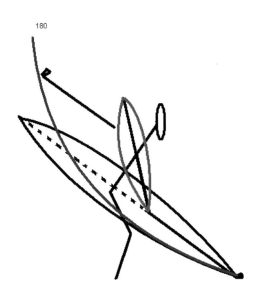

Notice how the golf club starts on the club arc, which is the black arc. As the club works up the arm arc marked in red, it leaves the black arc. Before reaching the 180° position, the club parallels the same position of the club at the address position. The club works on an arc between the arm arc and the original shaft line. Rolling the wrist keeps the club on the blue line. The red arc is produced by pulling back the right shoulder on the backswing as the arms swing up. At the top of the backswing, the hands are above and behind the shoulders, and the club shaft will be parallel to the target line. The downswing should include the hands swinging down behind the shoulder as the wrist unrolls and the body turns through to face the target. The blue arc is the best arc to follow because it is balanced, which provides predictability and center hitting of the ball and clubface.

BEFORE THE 180° POSITION

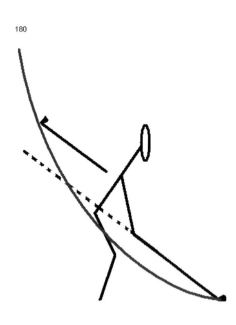

When the club is in a position above the hips, but before the 180° position, it will be parallel to the original shaft line. This means the butt end of the club will be pointing above the ball at this time. The reason the club gets in this position is because the club swings on the single arc of the arms. The club itself does not swing on a single arc; if it did then the shaft would point   at the ball at this moment. The shaft will parallel it's original line at least 6 times when swinging like the shape of golf.

THE 180° POSITION

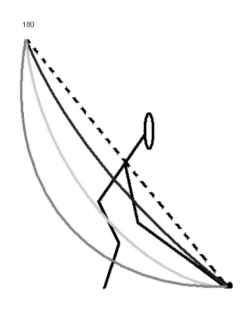

360° is a full circle. The club swings in a circular motion. The 180° position is one of two points that make a perfect swing. The second point is the pivot point. When the 2 points are used in the right combination a perfect swing is made. How the club reaches the 180° position is of no relevance on the backswing, just so it gets there. After this point the club changes direction. The full swing position is generally just past the 180° position. Some professional golfers use the purple arc, which is the most direct way to the 180° position. The purple arc is a single arc, but not a balanced arc. Players who use the purple arc need to re-route to the green line on the downswing, which is the balanced arc. While other players use the gray line on the backswing, they also need to use the green line on the downswing, which is the balance arc and the key to hitting the ball with the middle of the clubface. Generally, more golfers use vertical swings instead of flatter or horizontal swings because a lot of the golf instruction to this point has been based on a single arc mentality. Using the green line is the only way the impact of the club head on the ball can be consistently perfect.

PIVOT POINT

The pivot point is the single most important point in the golf swing. It determines the angle of compression, which allows the loft of the club to determine the height of the ball flight. Without it, the ball may have a tough time getting airborne, even with a perfect backswing and downswing. There are two pivot points. One is the top of the left leg, and another is the moment the club returns back to the inside of the target line on the follow-through.

When the body turns through, it rotates over the top of the left leg. This rotation should be as level as possible with the shoulders. The shoulders, hips, and arms should all be working together, and nothing should be independent of the others. Here is how to to get a feeling of the pivot, place the left elbow above the left hip, grab the left wrist with the right hand. Rotate the hips through, and notice that the arm is along for the ride. Don't move the arms separate from the body. Everything must move in one unit. Do this to get a feeling for a pivot. (check pictures)

Another way to get the club to the inside of the target line is to roll the wrist on the follow-through of the swing. But if the wrist roll is too quick, the ball will curve to the left (called a hook).

Hip pivot in combination with wrist roll optimizes the pivot point.

31

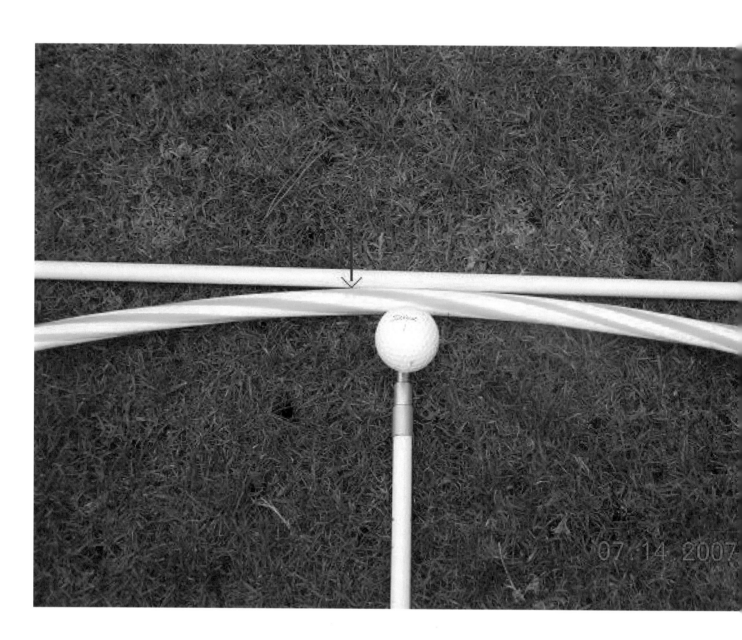

32

33

34

36

40

41

43

44

Golfers don't need a perfect swing to play the game of golf. But to play well it is difficult with a poor swing shape. No other shape of the golf swing has as high of a probability for perfect shots. Matching the right shape with the right posture and grip allows golfers to reach their fullest potential. Hopefully you found this description of the golf swing to follow a logical progression. I know it will help your game the closer you achieve the shape of golf plane and simple. Happy golfing. Bob Haas

49

CPSIA information can be obtained
at www.ICGtesting.com
Printed in the USA
LVIC04n2105201216
518146LV00007B/8